W9-BTP-343

If I Were a Kid in Ancient Egypt

Cricket Books

Peterborough, NH

J
932
I23

Staff

Editorial Director: Lou Waryncia
Editor: Ken Sheldon
Book Design: David Nelson, www.dnelsondesign.com
Designer: Ann Dillon
Proofreader: Eileen Terrill

Text Credits

The content of this volume is derived from articles that first appeared in *AppleSeeds* and *Calliope* magazines. Contributing writers: Mariam Ayad, Robert Steven Bianchi, Edward Brovarski, Joann J. Burch, Diana Childress, Stephen Currie, Cyndy Hall, Joyce Haynes, Holly Hutto, Leonard H. Lesko, Jane Hill McHugh, Bonnie McMeans, Cari Meister, Catharine H. Roehrig, Jane Scherer, Emily Teeter, Susan Washburn, Peggy Wilgus Wymore, Jennifer Wegner.

Picture Credits

Photos.com: Cover; Photo-Objects.net: Cover; Shutterstock: Cover, 8, 9, 19, 25, 26, 27, 28; Clipart.com: 6, 15, 17; The Art Archive/Dagli Orti: 7; Scala/Art Resource, NY: 14; Egyptian National Museum, Cairo, Egypt/Bridgeman Art Library © Boltin Picture Library: 24.

Illustration Credits

Dan Daly: 4–5, 12–13; Lynn Jeffery: 10–11; Barbara Paxson: 16; Doug Van Fleet: 18; Holly Hutto: 20; Cheryl Jacobsen: 21, 29.

Library of Congress Cataloging-in-Publication Data

If I were a kid in ancient Egypt / Lou Waryncia, editorial director ; Ken Sheldon, editor. — 1st ed.

   p. cm. — (Children of the ancient world)

   Includes index.

   ISBN-13: 978-0-8126-7932-8 (hardcover)

   ISBN-10: 0-8126-7932-6 (hardcover)

1. Egypt—Social life and customs—To 332 B.C.—Juvenile literature.
2. Children—Egypt—Juvenile literature.
I. Waryncia, Lou. II. Sheldon, Kenneth M. III. Series.

   DT61.I35 2006

   932—dc22   2006014672

Copyright © 2006 Carus Publishing Company

All rights reserved. No part of this publication may be reproduced in whole or in part, or stored in a retrieval system, or transmitted in any form or by any means, electronic, mechanical, photocopying, recording, or otherwise, without the written permission of the publisher. For information regarding permission, write to Carus Publishing, 30 Grove Street, Peterborough, NH 03458.

Cricket Books

a division of Carus Publishing

30 Grove Street, Suite C

Peterborough, NH 03458

www.cricketmag.com

Printed in China

Table of Contents

A Kid's Life

magine you are growing up in ancient Egypt during the age of the pyramids, about 4,500 years ago. What is your life like? You probably spend a lot of time with your family. Most children don't go to school, since only a few people know how to read and write.

Your head is likely shaved, except for one lock of hair worn over the right ear. And you don't worry about clothes because you don't wear any!

Whether you are rich or poor, your house is probably made of mud bricks. The size of your house will depend on your father's job. Is he the king of Egypt, known as the pharaoh? Then your home is a palace with many rooms, though still made of mud bricks. Is he a nobleman or a scribe (one of the few people who could write)? In that case, your house may have a private courtyard with flowers and a fish pond.

If you live in the capital city of Memphis, your father or mother might be a weaver who makes cloth. Maybe they work in a bakery, making bread. In that case, you live in a small house, close to others like yours, with doors that open to a dusty, narrow street.

Life on a Farm

But most likely your father is a farmer. If he is a rich farmer, you may live on a huge farm along the Nile River. If he has a small farm, you may live in a tiny town near the fields.

All the houses have flat roofs. Because of Egypt's hot weather, your family often goes to the roof in the evening to get cool. You may even sleep on the roof.

Wherever you live, it is on the sand. Except for a narrow strip of land along the Nile, everyplace is sand. The green land along the river is too precious to build houses on. It's the only place to grow all of the food for the country.

Because growing crops is so important, most families farm. At harvest time, everyone helps. Your job may be to tie up the shafts of wheat and put them into bundles.

If your father is a farmer, he does not work from June

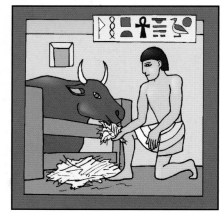

to September. The Nile floods its banks then, and all of the farmland is covered with water. At that time the pharaoh may order your father to work for him. If not, you have vacation time. Then you might take a boat trip down the Nile with your family. Or you might walk to the next village for a visit, with a donkey carrying your supplies.

Whatever the season, religion is an important part of your life. You probably believe in many gods and wear an amulet or figure of one of them on a necklace. Your parents say this protects you from evil and illness.

Childhood is carefree and happy, but it is short. By the time you are a young teenager, you'll be married. After that, you'll be expected to live your life just as your parents have lived theirs.

Egypt's Kingdoms

Ancient Egypt had a long history, from about 3000 B.C. to 341 B.C. Historians have divided that history into various periods, the most important of which are: the Old Kingdom (or the Age of Pyramids, from around 2686 to 2181 B.C.); the Middle Kingdom (from about 2040 to 1782 B.C.); and the New Kingdom (or the Age of Conquest, from 1570 to 1085 B.C.)

Well-Dressed Egyptians

If you lived in ancient Egypt, your ideas about clothing would be different from ours today.

During most of the year, the weather in Egypt is very warm, and Egyptians dressed—or undressed—to suit the climate. Children of both sexes ran around naked until they reached puberty. Even some adults went naked, including farm workers, fishermen, and fowlers (people who hunt birds).

The clothes that Egyptians did wear were simple and cool. Men wore a short linen skirt wrapped around their waist like a bath towel and fastened with a belt. Women wore long dresses, with plain or beaded shoulder straps.

Both men and women wore their hair very short, though they wore wigs on formal occasions. For men, facial hair was limited to a trim mustache or a short chin beard. Most men seem to have shaved their bodies as well.

If you were a kid in ancient Egypt, your entire head would be shaved, except for one lock of hair on the side. But at least you wouldn't have to worry about picking up your clothes!

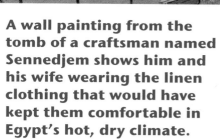

A wall painting from the tomb of a craftsman named Sennedjem shows him and his wife wearing the linen clothing that would have kept them comfortable in Egypt's hot, dry climate.

Great Feats

The ancient Egyptians came up with many great ideas, such as the sundial, mummification, cement, the decimal system (counting by tens), and glassmaking. Here are a few more of their great ideas and inventions.

Stairway to Heaven?

The biggest achievements of ancient Egyptians are the

pyramids, tombs for the mummified bodies of the dead pharaohs. The largest of these is the Great Pyramid, the only one of the Seven Wonders of the World still standing. No one knows for sure, but the shape of pyramids may represent the slanting rays of the sun, or a stairway to heaven that the dead king could climb to the sky.

Plant to Paper

The ancient Egyptians made a type of paper out of papyrus, a reed that grew along the Nile River. Writing on paper was a lot easier than writing on stone or wood, and more portable! Papyrus made it easier to do business, and it came to be used throughout the ancient world.

Buds to Duds

Another plant that grew along the banks of the Nile was flax. The Egyptians figured out how to turn flax into cloth. They spun the fibers from flax into threads, then wove the threads into linen, just as we do today. They used the linen for clothes, mummy wrappings, bed sheets, tapestries, and sails, among other things.

Water Works

Egyptians were among the first people to use irrigation, bringing water to dry land through channels or pipes. Every year, the Nile overflowed its banks and water flowed across the fields. But sometimes this was too much water and sometimes too little. They dug canals with dams that let them control the flow of water and take it to areas the floodwaters usually did not reach. Without irrigation, the civilization of ancient Egypt would not have been possible.

Mind Your Manners!

Don't chew with your mouth open! Use your fork, not your fingers! Sit up straight!

Does this sound like your dinner table? Parents have been telling kids how to act at the dinner table for thousands of years. But if you lived in ancient Egypt, your table manners would be different than they are today. Ancient Egyptians had their own rules about how to behave while eating.

Imagine that you are at an ancient Egyptian meal. Everyone is sitting on a big reed mat. Your mother sets the fish down in the middle of the mat. Your father pours the beer. You and your pet monkey are just about to begin when your mother fires off the rules—for what seems like the millionth time this week.

Dip your hands!

Ancient Egyptians washed their hands before they ate. They did not use a bathroom or kitchen sink. They dipped their hands in bowls of water.

Eat with your fingers!

Ancient Egyptians did not use silverware. Most people ate with their fingers.

Don't stare at your food!

Only people with bad manners stared at their food— even if it was hyena meat!

Don't feed scraps to the monkey!

Ancient Egyptians kept many pets, including monkeys, cats, dogs, and birds. We can only guess that feeding from the table was a no-no.

Save your scraps for the goat!

In ancient Egypt everything was recycled. Nothing was thrown away. Any leftover food was fed to the animals.

Family Time

Ancient Egyptian families liked to have fun together. A favorite outing was to go fishing and hunting in the marshes. These are wet, grassy areas along the river or in the delta. (The delta is the place in northern Egypt where the Nile River fans out into many smaller waterways.)

The whole family would climb into a boat made from reeds and sail through the marshes. Children picked lotus blossoms and caught fish with spears or nets. Sometimes the family used throwing sticks to hunt wild birds.

Egypt's many festivals were a special time for families. There were festivals for the beginning of spring, the harvest, and the flooding of the Nile River. There were festivals for the birth, death, or crowning of a pharaoh.

At festival time tents and food stalls were set up. People feasted on watermelons, grapes, pomegranates, figs, and little loaves of bread. Sometimes drummers in feathered costumes came from the lands far south of the desert. Bands of young girls played the lute, harp, or flute, and women shook the sistrum (a sacred rattle). Acrobats

danced to the music, did back bends, and turned somersaults.

Fun at the Festivals

In the city of Thebes, the Feast of Opet lasted for nearly a month. It took place during the time that the Nile River flooded the fields. No one could work during that time, so people came to Thebes to enjoy the fun.

The Opet Feast began when priests carried a golden statue of a special god out of Karnak Temple. They placed the statue in the middle of a beautiful boat. People crowded the riverbanks to watch the boat sail by. It was a time when Egyptians could beg the gods and pharaoh for favors.

In the Festival of the Valley, the Egyptians honored their dead relatives and ancestors. They wanted to make sure that the spirits of the dead enjoyed a good life after death. Families visited their ancestors' tombs to make offerings of food and drink. Then they feasted in chapels above the tombs. Afterward they spent the night in the chapels to be close to the souls of their dead relatives. To ancient Egyptians, family was all-important, whether dead or alive!

Playtime & Pets

Young King Tut liked senet so much that he was buried with four of the game boards.

Imagine you are a kid in ancient Egypt with nothing to do one afternoon. A friend suggests a game of tug of war, arm wrestling, or a board game. In ancient Egypt? That's right. Lots of games that we play today are similar to games Egyptian children played thousands of years ago.

On the walls of Egyptian tombs are pictures of children

playing games like leapfrog and "ring around the rosy." There are scenes of children wrestling and giving each other piggyback rides. A favorite game was foot-grabbing. To play, a group of children would sit in a circle, with one child in the center. Those in the circle gently nudged the boy or girl in the center with their feet. The person in the center tried to catch hold of someone's foot. If your foot was caught, it was your turn to grab feet.

Favorite toys of Egyptian children included colorful leather or clay balls, spinning tops, wooden pull-along animals with movable parts, and dolls with string or bead hair. These toys were made from leather, clay, wood, ivory, and dried mud.

Archaeologists have even found board games in the tombs. One of these is called senet, a game somewhat like checkers, chess, or backgammon. Senet was so popular that four game boards were found in King Tut's tomb!

A Passion for Pets

The ancient Egyptians were also very fond of pets. Their most popular dog looked like a modern greyhound and was used for hunting. Green and red monkeys were also popular as pets, for people who could afford them. Baboons were less popular, perhaps because they could be aggressive and sometimes turned nasty.

Egyptian scenes of daily life often show young children holding a pet bird or two by the wings. A favorite bird was the hoopoe, which had an orange body, black-and-white wings, and black-tipped crest.

cats favorite pet

But the most popular pets among the ancient Egyptians were cats. In fact, they worshipped cats! Besides being pets, cats helped protect the Egyptians' food supply by catching mice and rats. They also helped their masters on fowling (bird-hunting) expeditions.

Cats and Gods

One cat owner, the son of Pharaoh Amenhotep III, loved his cat so much that he had a special stone coffin made for its burial.

The Egyptians associated several animals with gods and goddesses. The god Horus could appear as a falcon, the god Sobek as a crocodile, and the goddess Hathor as a cow. But the cat was special. It was connected with both gods and goddesses. The most important of these was Bastet, the cat goddess of childbirth. Egyptian parents would travel to the temple of Bastet to gain her blessing for the birth of a child or to thank her for a healthy new daughter or son. And how did they thank her? Often with a mummified cat!

The priests of Bastet actually selected a living cat to represent the goddess. This cat was pampered all its life, and when it died, it received a sumptuous burial. After the funeral, the priests searched Egypt for a new cat. This cat became the new symbol of Bastet until it died, and the cycle was repeated.

Doctor's Orders

Has your doctor ever treated you with cucumbers? He might have, if you lived in long-ago Egypt.

Ancient Egypt was famous for its doctors. Their knowledge has been preserved in long papyrus documents that describe how to examine a patient, what the doctor should expect to find, and how an illness was to be treated.

Egyptian doctors were trained in anatomy, but there were many things they didn't understand about the human body. For example, they thought the heart was where our thoughts and emotions came from, rather than the brain. They were very skilled in dealing with injuries of all kinds, but they didn't know about germs or bacteria.

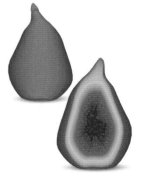

Figs

An Egyptian doctor could choose from a large number of prescriptions for treating illnesses. These medicines used more than 600 different ingredients, including myrrh (a gum resin), malachite (a green mineral), dung, blood, fat from various animals, figs, dates, aloe, cucumbers, dill, and mustard.

Egyptian medicine was a mixture of science and magic. Doctors chose many of the ingredients for prescriptions because they resembled the cure somehow. For example, they used crushed ostrich eggs to treat a fractured skull and the blood of a black calf to prevent hair from turning gray. And they often recited spells while performing a medical procedure.

Malachite

School Days

In ancient Egypt, only the very smartest children went to school, where they learned to be scribes. Scribes were very important people, since they were almost the only ones who could read and write.

Most scribes were men, although records tell us that there were a few women scribes. Boys entered scribal school when they were quite young and studied hard for about 10 to 12 years.

Why did it take so long to learn to read and write? Because ancient Egyptians used picture signs called hieroglyphs to write their language. Some hieroglyphs stood for objects such as a tree or a house. Others stood for sounds, which made up words just like the letters of our alphabet.

There were about 800 commonly used hieroglyphs, and it took years to learn them all. Scribes also had to know how to write hieratic, a kind of shorthand script used for everyday writing.

Students memorized the hieroglyphic signs and practiced writing by copying things that had

These hieroglyphs were carved on a wall at the Temple of Kom Ombo in Egypt.

already been written: letters, literature, religious records, and business and government documents. As they copied, they learned about more than just their language.

Scribal students used writing tools similar to a watercolor set you might have today. But instead of many colors, scribes used only red and black. They carried small pots of water to mix with the inks. Their brushes, made of reed plants, were held in a small case. The hieroglyph that means "scribe" is made up of those three elements—brushes, a water pot, and ink disks.

Students practiced writing on flat pieces of limestone, a kind of rock that could be found everywhere in Egypt. Archaeologists have found many examples of student exercises written on these flakes of stone.

Sometimes a student or a scribe needed to write something very important. Then he wrote on papyrus.

Parents were happy to pay the high price to send a child to scribal school because it meant he could get a good job when he grew up. He might be a doctor, a

Hist-O-Bit
Hieroglyphs could be written from left to right, right to left, or even top to bottom.

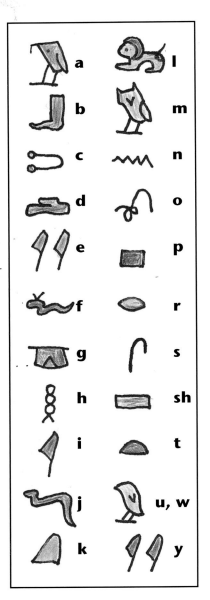

a		l
b		m
c		n
d		o
e		p
f		r
g		s
h		sh
i		t
j		u, w
k		y

Although some hieroglyphs stood for objects, others represented sounds that made up words, just like our alphabet.

priest, the secretary to a noble family, or the boss of a group of workers.

Hieroglyphs were used for about 3,500 years. Then, about 1,300 years ago, Egyptians stopped using them, and their meaning was lost. No one knew what the words carved on stone sculptures and painted on the walls of tombs meant.

Then, in about 1822, a French scholar named Jean-François Champollion figured out how to decode hieroglyphs. He used an ancient tablet called the Rosetta Stone, which contained the same message in three different types of writing: ancient Greek, a kind of hieratic script, and hieroglyphs. Since Champollion could read Greek, he was able to translate the hieroglyphs. The age-old mystery of hieroglyphs was finally solved.

By the Numbers

The ancient Egyptians used numbers that looked very different from ours. For the number 1, they wrote the symbol I. ∩ meant 10. And the symbol ℓ was 100. To make numbers up to 9, Egyptians just strung Is together. I I I was 3, I I I I I I I was 7, and I I I I was 4.

To write the number 362, an Egyptian student would have had to write ℓℓℓ∩∩∩∩∩∩II. Doing math homework must have taken forever!

Making Papyrus

magine you are a scribe in ancient Egypt. You have your brushes, your inks, and your water pot. Now all you need is some papyrus to write on. So how do you make papyrus?

First you need papyrus plants. Begin by cutting the stem of the papyrus plant into pieces about 9 inches long.

Now slice the pieces into thin strips.

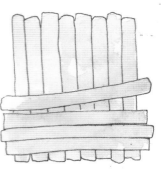

Lay the strips side by side on a flat surface. Then place another layer of strips across the first layer.

Hammer these layers flat and leave them to dry in the sun. The sticky juices from the plant act like glue to hold the sheet together. Once the sheet is dry, cut the edges to make them even.

Now glue several sheets together, end to end. This makes one long piece. Your papyrus is ready to be written on, rolled into a cylinder, tied with a string, and sealed.

Bread, Bees, & Beer

What did children eat in ancient Egypt? Did their parents make them finish their vegetables before dessert? Was there any candy? Did kids have peanut butter and jelly sandwiches 4,000 years ago?

No one knows for sure if kids in ancient Egypt had to eat all their vegetables. But the ruins of tombs and old houses give us clues about how the Egyptians ate.

Families in ancient Egypt grew their own food. They planted beans, lentils, onions, leeks, cucumbers, and other crops. Farmers often took heads of "sacred lettuce" to temples to thank the gods for a good harvest.

Fruit trees were everywhere. Children picked their own dates, figs, and pomegranates for afternoon snacks.

The Egyptians were the world's first beekeepers. They kept hives in large pottery jars and fearlessly brushed the bees aside to collect their honeycombs.

The honey was stored in covered containers. Children must have enjoyed dipping their fingers into these bowls for a sweet treat.

Ancient Egypt's main food was bread, and the Egyptians ate it at every meal. There were many different kinds of bread, in lots of shapes and sizes. Some recipes used fruits, garlic, or nuts to flavor the loaves.

Eating bread caused some problems, though. Bits of desert sand and stones often got into the dough. Scientists have discovered that most Egyptian mummies have worn and missing teeth. They believe the Egyptians wore their teeth down while chewing on their bread.

The Egyptians did not sit at dining tables the way we do. Instead, they sat on mats on the floor and ate from their own small tables.

Most people ate two meals a day, morning and evening, though the wealthy may have eaten three meals a day. Average families might eat goat and sheep meat occasionally, but the rich often ate ibex (wild goat), antelope, deer, rabbit, and even hyena!

Both rich and poor people ate wild ducks and geese, which they captured during the migration season in the fall. They also ate pigeons, doves, and quail, along with their eggs. Of course, the Nile River provided Egyptians with lots of fish, but fish was mostly eaten by poor people.

Since they didn't have refrigerators or freezers, the Egyptians dried their meat in the sun so that it would last longer.

The Egyptians invented beer, and everyone drank it, from rich to poor. Wine was more expensive, and only the upper classes drank it. While exploring ancient tombs, archaeologists have found 4,500-year-old beer jars, with the dried beer still inside. Egyptians didn't go anywhere without their beer!

Hist-O-Bit

Instead of peanut butter and jelly sandwiches, kids in ancient Egypt spread their bread with garlic and raw onions. Maybe that's why they also chewed mint leaves to sweeten their breath!

The Boy King

Pharaoh
Tutankhamun was
ruler of all Egypt,
and the people
believed he was a god. He wore
a bull's tail on his belt that
showed his strength, and a
false beard as a symbol of
power. His word was law.
And he was only 9 years old.
Young Tutankhamun—
sometimes called King Tut—
became pharaoh when his
father, the pharaoh before him,
died. Because he was so young,
advisors helped him rule, and they
held great power. But Tutankhamun
was still the king of Egypt.

Tutankhamun had a brief
but successful reign. His most
important work was the restoration
of the temples of the old gods, which
had been neglected during his father's
reign. Unfortunately, he died suddenly,
before he could complete any major
building works. When he died, he was

only 18 years old. Egyptologists (people who study ancient Egypt) suspect that the young pharaoh might have been murdered. We don't know the truth. But in his death he has told us a great deal about his life.

Egyptologists discovered Tutankhamun's tomb in 1922. Inside the tomb, they found many objects that told them about the life of the young pharaoh. There were golden statues and cases of jewels. There were models of boats to carry the pharaoh on the Nile and models of servants to help him. Although most Egyptians drank beer, it seems likely that Tutankhamun did not like beer, since he had none in his tomb.

The tomb also held many things from Tutankhamun's childhood: small gloves that he had probably worn as a child, brightly colored balls, his senet games, and a wooden cat with a jaw that moved and a tail that wagged. We also know that he liked to hunt, because bows and arrows were buried with him.

Tutankhamun lived and died more than 3,300 years ago. Can you imagine what it would be like to rule all of Egypt when you were only 9 years old?

This magnificent mask (above) covered the head and shoulders of the mummified King Tut. An Egyptian artist fashioned the head of young Tutankhamun (opposite) to appear as if it were emerging from a lotus flower.

It's a Wrap!

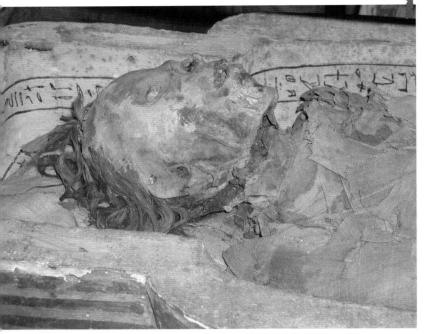

The ancient Egyptians mummified human bodies—like this one from the Royal Ontario Museum—as well as those of cats and other animals.

The ancient Egyptians believed that a person's spirit continued to exist after death. They imagined that this existence was similar to life on earth. So they thought they had to provide the spirit with food, shelter, clothing, and anything else that living people need. Since those things can decay, they also provided longer-lasting substitutes made of wood or stone, along with images painted or carved on the tomb walls.

One of the most important burial rituals was mummification, their method of preserving the corpse. Although the Egyptians believed the spirit could exist outside the body after death, they thought it needed to return "home" every once in a while.

The oldest mummies in Egypt come from the prehistoric period, before about 3200 B.C. Back then, the Egyptians buried their dead without any coffin, in the desert that surrounds the farmland on either side of the Nile River. Some of the corpses were preserved by the natural drying effect of the desert heat.

Later, the Egyptians began wrapping bodies in yards of linen bandages. But this method did nothing to preserve the body, which usually decomposed inside the wrappings.

Eventually, the Egyptians learned to use chemicals to help preserve the body. They also realized that the internal organs decomposed more quickly than the rest of the corpse. They began removing the lungs, liver, stomach, and intestines and preserving them separately.

Then they packed the corpse with bags of natron, a type of salt mined in the desert. The salt was left in place for several weeks to dry out the body. After the salt was removed, the corpse was rubbed with ointments and oils to prevent the dried skin from cracking.

After that, to restore the body's shape, the embalmers stuffed it with sawdust or wads of linen. Then they wrapped it, sometimes using as much as 500 yards of linen bandages.

The Egyptians practiced mummification this way—drying the body, restoring its shape, and then wrapping it—for more than 2,000 years.

Hist-O-Bit

The smallest animal embalmed by the Egyptians was an insect, a scarab beetle found buried in its own limestone mummy case.

Wrapping a typical mummy required hundreds of yards of linen.

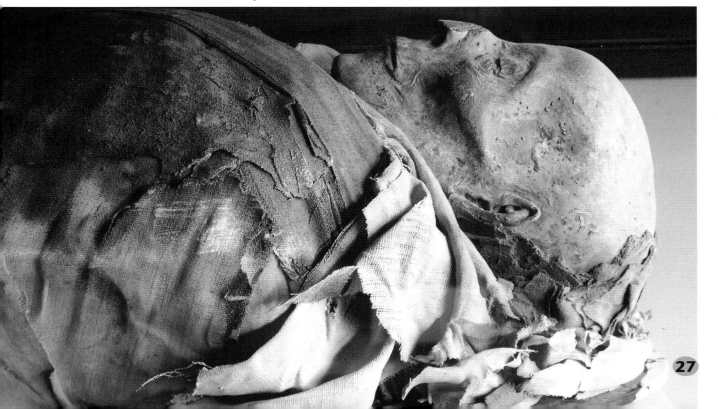

Great Gods of Egypt

The gods of Egypt often changed over the course of its history. Here are some important gods of Egypt's Old Kingdom.

Anubis—the jackal-headed guardian of the cemetery, associated with embalming.

Hathor—a sky goddess, represented as a cow, associated with rebirth and foreign lands.

Horus—the falcon-headed god of the sky who protected the king.

Isis—mother goddess, the sister and wife of Osiris.

Min—god of fertility.

Neith—goddess of hunting.

Osiris—most famous of all Egyptian gods, the king of the dead and the judge in the underworld.

Re—god of the sun, considered to be the king and father of the gods.

Seth—god of the desert, often referred to as the god of confusion.

Thoth—the ibis-headed god of wisdom and writing.

Statues and images of Anubis, the god of embalming, are often found in tombs and pyramids. Here, Anubis holds the ankh, symbol of eternal life, in his right hand.

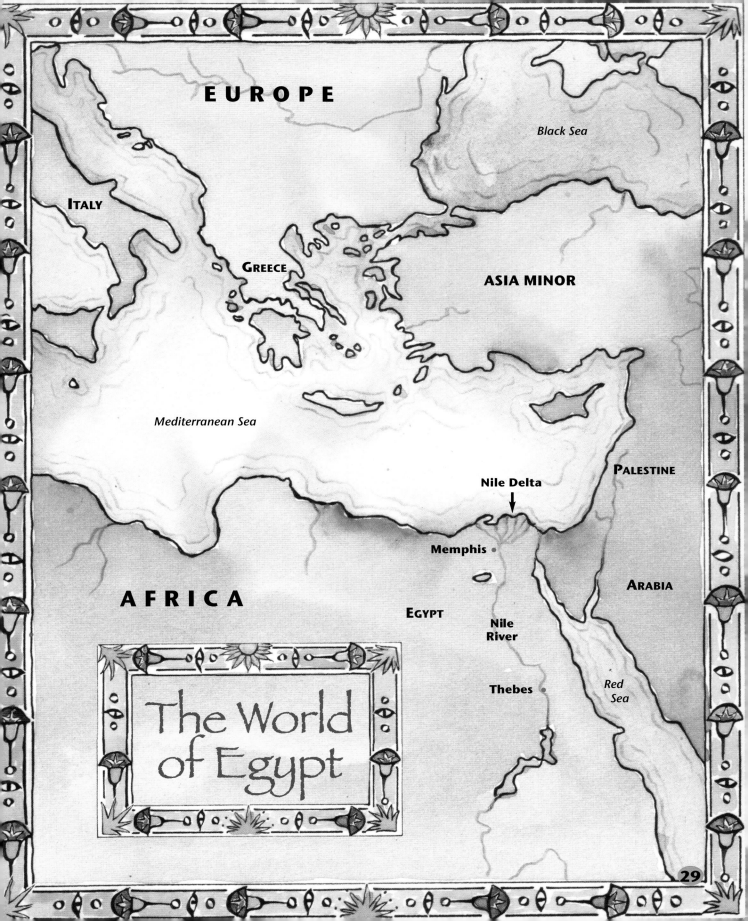

EUROPE

Black Sea

ITALY

GREECE

ASIA MINOR

Mediterranean Sea

PALESTINE

Nile Delta

Memphis •

ARABIA

AFRICA

EGYPT

Nile
River

Thebes •

Red
Sea

The World
of Egypt

Glossary

Anatomy The study of the structure of animals and plants.

Archaeologist A person who studies ancient times by exploring fossils, relics, and ruins.

Decimal system The system of counting based on the number 10.

Delta A fertile area where the mouth of a river empties into a larger body of water and where floods may often occur.

Egyptologist A person who studies ancient Egypt.

Flax A plant used to make linen.

Fowler A person who hunts birds.

Hieratic Shorthand writing used by ancient Egyptian scribes for everyday writing.

Hieroglyphs Symbols used in ancient Egyptian writing.

Hoopoe A colorful bird popular as a pet in ancient Egypt.

Ibex A type of wild goat with long horns that curve backward.

Ibis A wading bird with a long, thin, curved bill.

Irrigation Transportation of water to dry land through channels or pipes.

Leek A vegetable like a small onion but with long dark-green leaves.

Limestone A kind of rock used by the Egyptians for writing exercises.

Linen Cloth woven from the fibers of the flax plant.

Mummification The process of preserving a dead body developed by the Egyptians.

Natron A type of salt used in mummification.

Nile River The longest river in the world, which runs the length of Egypt and was crucial to its development.

Papyrus A kind of paper made from the papyrus plant, which grew in the marshes along the Nile.

Pharaoh The ruler of ancient Egypt.

Rosetta Stone An ancient tablet with writing in Greek, hieratic script, and hieroglyphs, which helped translate hieroglyphic writing.

Scribe A person who had been trained to read and write.

Senet An Egyptian board game in which two players throw dice and move pieces along a zigzag track.

Seven Wonders of the World The most notable human-made structures of ancient times, including the Hanging Gardens of Babylon, the Mausoleum at Halicarnassus, the temple of Artemis at Ephesus, the statue called the Colossus of Rhodes, the statue of Zeus by Phidias at Olympia, the Pharos (lighthouse) at Alexandria, and the Great Pyramid at Giza (the only one still in existence).

Sistrum A rattle used in sacred rituals.

Index

If I Were A Kid
in the Ancient World…

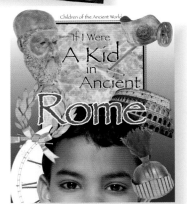

What games would I play?
Would I have a pet?
Would I go to school?

Just like kids today, kids of the ancient world played with friends, had pets, went to school, and learned life lessons from their parents. In fact, many of the things kids use and experience today resemble those from ancient times.

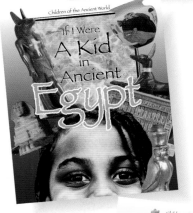

Each book in the Children of the Ancient World series looks at what life was like for kids in the ancient regions of Egypt, Greece, Rome, and China. Comparing and contrasting life of kids now as to then, this series presents solidly researched information in a clear, exciting manner that will inspire and attract young readers. Each book is perfect for research or pursuing an emerging interest in the life of ancient times.

Titles in the Children of the Ancient World series

If I Were a Kid in Ancient Greece	APP67929
If I Were a Kid in Ancient Rome	APP67930
If I Were a Kid in Ancient Egypt	APP67932
If I Were a Kid in Ancient China	APP67931

$17.95 each
Order Code: SA21

Cricket Books
www.cricketmag.com
800-821-0115

Our books are available through all major wholesalers as well as directly from us.